AN

ORATION,

DELIVERED BEFORE THE

CITIZENS *of* PORTLAND,

AND THE

SUPREME JUDICIAL COURT

OF THE

COMMONWEALTH OF MASSACHUSETTS,

ON THE

Fourth day of July, 1799;

BEING THE ANNIVERSARY OF

AMERICAN INDEPENDENCE.

⸺⬥⬥⬥⸺

BY A. STODDARD.

⸺⬥⬥⬥⸺

ENEMIES IN WAR—IN PEACE, FRIENDS.

DEC. AMER. INDEP.

PORTLAND:

PRINTED AND SOLD BY *E. A. JENKS.*

1799.

THE following ORATION *was* delivered, and *is* published, at the request of a respectable Committee of the town of *Portland*. Considering the temper of the times, and the dangers to which we are exposed, the Author has avoided the touches of rhetoric, and escaped the sallies of fancy:—Argumentation—the establishment and illustration of sound political principles, and an exposition of the deleterious nature of revolutionary policy, were the objects he had in view. Accustomed to reflect on the nature and extent of our foreign relations, and to watch their tendencies and vibrations, he has manifested considerable confidence on Governmental subjects ; and he has not, to his knowledge, made a material assertion respecting them without a substantial document in his possession to warrant it. Should the Author be so fortunate as to induce any deluded citizen to relinquish his political errors and herecies, an important object will be gained.

PORTLAND, JULY 4, 1799.

ORATION.

AMERICANS !

I T has hitherto been usual for orators, on
occasions similar to the present, to furnish labored dissertations on the nature of civil Government, and on
the origin of our political existence—to entertain their
hearers with animated descriptions of the progress of
freedom, and with diversified pictures of public peace
and prosperity. But at a period, when *Europe* is afflicted with terrible commotions, and exhibits a disgustful
scene of Gothic barbarity and blood—When *America*,
and the world, seem devoted to the same contagious
stamina of revolution, a serious aspect is imposed on this
anniversary, and demands rather the exercise of deliber-
ate judgment, than the spontaneous effusions of joy and
gratulation. Permit me then to touch lightly on the
painful history of our country—more fully to investigate the causes of national disorders, and the remedies
necessary to mitigate their asperity—to unfold and il-
lustrate the interest and policy of the *American* people,
and the destructive tendency of modern revolutionary
sentiments. The method here prescribed is consistent
with the portentous crisis of the times, and compatible
with the practice of the fires of antiquity, in the sanctuary of the GODS.

IT is a fixed principle in the economy of nature, that nations, like families, must divide, and occupy separate portions of the globe. Excessive population, and a dissimilarity of political and religious sentiments, not unfrequently contribute to this end. Add to this—mankind possess an invincible propensity to emigration ; they figure to themselves riches and pleasures in the desert waste, and pastoral and romantic scenes, not to be found in populous cities, nor in cultivated countries. Were it not for this propensity, nature would be frustrated in the dispersion of her children—in the birth and progress of culture, and in the diffusion of the arts and sciences.

THIS remark is forcibly exemplified, in the discovery, settlement, and progressive improvement of *America*. History furnishes us with no character similar to that of our own. Most nations owe their origin to the conquests, or to the accidental settlements of barbarians ; the early events of whom are either unknown, or inveloped in fable. The first emigrants to this country were advanced in civilization, and were acquainted with the arts and conveniences of life : They possessed a wakeful jealousy of arbitrary rule ; always ready to defend their rights—cool, dispassionate, and brave. This character they inherited as a legacy from the early inhibitants of *Britain* ; whose sagacity and exertion enabled them to set bounds to the dangerous prerogatives of the crown, and to live in a state of freedom. What but this awakened such a formidable opposition to the legions of imperial *Rome* ? What but this established the great charter of privileges in 1215—a transcript of the rights enjoyed under the more ancient Saxon monarchs ? What but this produced the religious reformation in 1559—the celebrated petition of right in 1628, and ultimately, the memorable revolution in 1688, at the accession of the House of Orange to the throne ?

BUT *England*, like all other countries, exhibits in her history, many periods of weakness, and of cruelty—

especially when she sharpened the dagger, and lighted the torch, of fanaticism ; and when, with the rod of tyranny, she wasted the human race. In some portions of the fifteenth and sixteenth centuries, she was transformed into a slaughter-house of heretics, and trembled with the agonies of malefactors at the stake. We are accustomed to look with horror on these brutal excesses of arbitrary power, and to stand astonished at the patience and depravity of man. Some doubt the benevolence, and even the existence of Deity ; and they derive it from, and fortify it by, the prevalence of physical and moral evil—from the apparent disorders of nature, and from the conflicts of nations : But these painful vicissitudes are not without a salutary use in the Divine Government of the universe. Men of this temper heed not the *causes*, nor trace the *effects*, of such awful, tho' wise and necessary, dispensations of Providence. The mediated destruction of ROMULUS in his cradle, founded the *Roman* republic. To the conquest and pillage of *Europe* by the invincible CAESAR, we are indebted for civilization, and for a knowledge of the arts and sciences. The *American* empire owes its origin to the sanguinary tribunals of *Britain*, and its subsequent independence to the oppressive and arbitrary measures of her councils.

GREAT-BRITAIN has generally been celebrated for her political wisdom, and as the careful nurse of manly sentiment and virtue—yet we often find her under the domination of a crooked and disjointed policy, and disposed to establish the reign of despotism. Early in the present century, measures were concerted to deprive us of our rights. These rights were secured to us by various charters. These charters were considered by *England* as errors in her policy ; and she resolved to impair them by a gradual, and almost imperceptible assumption of authority over us. Hence our commerce in many instances was restricted, and in others totally prohibited. : Hence exorbitant excise and import duties were levied and collected with a greedy hand : Hence to cut down the pitch and tar trees of our forest—to manufacture steel, or to slit iron in our forges, exposed us to heavy penalties : Hence the common law of the land, and the trial by jury, were abolished, and our citizens obliged to answer to charges of a criminal nature, before a foreign tribunal : And then, as a prelude to hostilities on the one part, or to unconditional submission on the other, we were insulted with this pointed declaration, "*that Great-Britan had a right to bind us* "*in all cases whatsoever.*"

THIS tone of unwarranted authority, joined to repeated acts of aggression, awakened the pride and fortitude of *America*. Memorable is that day in our annals, when *Lexington* and *Concord* became the tombs of *English* glory ; and terrible to *Britain* was that day, when the heights of *Charlestown* were immersed in the blood of her veteran sons. To detail the events of the Revolution, would only be a trite display of historical erudition. We might excite a mixture of pity and resentment at the wanton cruelties and depredations of an enemy—and a deluge of tears at the recollection of departed heroes. But the events of the present day, of which we shall treat in the sequel, demand the suffrage of all these passions. Permit me only to say, that time has, in a great measure, closed the wounds, and repaired the ravages of war—that our citizens, who expired in the bed of honor, are set like stars of the first magnitude—and that to their memory a monument is erected, as durable as the pillars of time.

NO sooner had *Great-Britain* yielded to the claims of *America*, then the difficulties of a political nature succeeded to those of war. The singular genius of the *American* people required a form of Government, dissimilar to any in existence. We had found that systems, drawn from abstract theory, deceived us in their application to practice. The Confederation of the States was a transcript of the Amphystionic and Achean leagues of *Greece* ; and, like them, it contained the seeds of its own dissolution. The want of adequate powers in the federal head, and the imbecility of our fiscal arrangements, were among its most prominent defects. These primary errors in our policy, tho' extremely alarming in their nature, tended to stimulate our patriotism. They convinced us, that it is as difficult to imagine the operation of any political abstract theory, spun from the brain of a speculative philosopher, as it is to discover the qualities of a book by the title-page, or the propensities of the heart by the features of the face ; and that nations, if they mean to be happy, must be accommodated with systems of Government, adapted to their particular wants. Systems of Government are not reducible, like those of morals, to any fixed standard of right—they grow out of the errors of society—and their energies must operate in proportion to the ignorance or knowledge—the ferocity or humanity of mankind. Speculative writers, therefore, on the subject of Government, seldom derive their principles from actual experiment : They forsake the path marked out by the hand of nature—and place men in a situation, in which they ought to exist, rather than contemplate them in the sphere in which they actually move. Our present federal Government was founded in a conviction of these truths. It has avoided all abstract theory ; and as it was the result of combined wisdom, drawn from the sober lessons of experience, it may justly be stiled a new experiment in legislation. Under it, our wounded credit has been restored—our revenue augmented beyond any former example ; —dignity and energy are attached to our pubic councils, and the utmost security and freedom are afforded to the citizens.

BUT such is the economy of the wisest institutions, that very few have been able to promise themselves any considerable duration. Some have been destroyed by a contest for power—some by the prevalence of ignorance and superstition, and others are liable to subversion by the rage of occasional disorders in the human mind—which are not less fatal to nations than the plague to individuals. The world is at this moment afflicted with an inveterate and singular disease—malignant in its nature—contagious in its operation, and which constitutes a new article in the vocabulary of national calamities. Effectually to resist its progress, desperate remedies must be applied—otherwise all legitimate Government will receive an incurable wound, and every moral and religious sentiment be banished from the human mind. We pretend not accurately to investigate its origin— but I beg leave to draw your attention to some of the most rational conjectures on the subject.

AT the close of the last, and at the beginning of the present, century, a new description of speculative philosophers, made a conspicuous figure in the elder world. By them all Religion and Government were deemed the mere instruments of tyrants—designed to perpetuate their power, and to keep the people in the chains of vassalage. By their inflammatory writings, always plausible, and conceived with the nicest art, they enlisted the prejudices and passions of mankind, and excited a spirit of uneasiness and revolt. Their great object was, with the scythe of desolation, to equalize the world, and gradually to establish the primeval state of man. To effect this delusive scheme, they aimed to destroy the belief of a GOD—to corrupt the public mind by their herecies—and to bring the Ministers of Religion, and the chief magistrates of nations, into contempt. Not content with the diffusion of these principles thro' the medium of labored volumes, periodical essays, and pamphlets, they found means to exhibit them at theatres, and other public places, in all the charms of eloquent diction. These may be considered, perhaps, as the remote causes of the present disorders—but the origin of a regular digested system of revolution, grounded on the passions and vices of men, is of a more modern date.

SUCH was the number of disorganizers and atheists in *France* and *Germany*, about the middle of the present century, that they formed themselves into private associations, and cemented their union by the most solemn oaths. These societies had in them many men of literary talents—a horde of pamphleteers and punsters, and most of the influential editors of newspapers—all of whom were extremely dissolute in their characters—devoid of any fixed and permanent principles on the subjects of Government and Religion, and on whose consciences atheistic and sanguinary notions, made no terrible impression. To augment the number of their apostles and followers, and at the same time to deceive the world as to the nature and extent of their principles, they assumed the character of Masons.* They resorted not to rebellion and arms, the usual weapons of political changes, but confided wholly in the physical force of public opinion ; and to collect this physical force to a point, and to direct it to an object, they eventually usurped the empire of learning—became the proprietors of literary journals, and other important sources of information— foisted themselves into the government of Colleges and Academies—obtained an invincible control over the courts of justice—and, by a secret impulse, moulded all the measures of legislation. This secret and powerful influence, enabled them to corrupt the integrity and morals of *Europe* by the propagation of their political dogmas and atheistical creeds ; and, in case of detection, to avoid the punishment due to their crimes.

THESE surreptitious societies were awakened to the dictates of antecedent philosophers and atheists. They aimed, by a cautious and powerful process, to revive the pastoral and golden ages of antiquity ;—for they

---

* The existence of the societies of *Illuminati* has given rise to much speculation. Authors, although they agree as to the origin and nature of them, have not been sufficiently explicit on one point ; —a cursory perusal inculcates a belief (especially among the less informed part of the community, and among men of suspicious tempers and strong prejudices) that the masonic institution is pregnant with Atheistic and revolutionary sentiments. The Rev. Dr. MORSE, a pillar of adamant in the temple of Federalism, has imbibed this mistaken notion. The practice of Masons, and the principles they inculcate, will best explain their detestation of Atheism and revolution : These modern doctrines are directly opposed to their principles ;—and they will not fail to resist their progress.

12

held that no true happiness was to be acquired in civilized community—nor unless free from the restraints of
Government, and the fetters of religion. No wonder
that such sentiments should flatter the prejudices of mankind—excite the whirlwinds of sedition, and draw vast
multitudes into their fatal vortex. Every day witnessed
their deleterious effects, but nobody could penetrate
their cause. The contagion was universal—it spread
like the plague of old—it operated on the mind like a
subtle poison on the body, and no remedy appeared to
baffle the malady.

SUCH was the increase of this contagion, and such
the number and influence of its devotees, that they e-
ventually unmasked themselves more fully to the world.
At the commencement of the French Revolution, near
600 of these nocturnal clubs existed in the bosom of
France and *Germany*. As this event was generated by
the silent operation of their principles on the public
mind, its progress was hastened and embittered by every
possible exertion. The more effectively to form, and
to extend a destructive system of revolutionary war, and
thereby to reduce their preposterous theory to practice,
a deputation from most of them met in the dark conclave at
Paris, and organized themselves into a grand convention
of the lodges—over which the DUKE OF ORLEANS presided, and in which the celebrated MIRABEAU, and the present TALLEYRAND, sustained the next two offices of rank.
In this convention, the exact counterpart of the Alem-
bic of hell, dissertations on philosophy, and the modern
rights of man, composed their elegant debates : Pro-
jects of Utopian felicity, the abolition of all society and
Government, and the utter extinction of every species
of religion, were openly discussed and concerted : The
ambassadors of heaven were driven from their alters, and
either banished or destroyed—monarchs precipitated
from their thrones, and either massacred or bound in
fetters of iron. Add to this—the Jacobin society in
Paris, so famous in the history of the *French* Revolution, was wholly composed of the members of this deputation ; and hence the origin of that detestable cha-

racter, so odious in all countries, and which is now considered as a reproach to human nature.

TO impute the disorders in *Europe* to the influence of these secret societies, is a sentiment of recent date ; and therefore the more liable to objection. But the acquisition of their records, and other documents—the testimony of repentant brethren, and the apparent homage paid them by the National Convention of *France*, establish the fact beyond the reach of doubt. Some of the early decrees of this convention against religious institutions, were palpable plagiaries from the homilies of these secret societies. They all, in the very same language, denounced the holy bible as a system of riddles and superstition : In the very same language, they all abolished the worship of GOD—the rites of the sanctuary—and the observation of the Sabbath ; and, in the very same language, they all recommended Atheism as the established creed of mankind. This affinity discovers itself in a vast variety of other interior operations. We see it even in the geometrical divisions of *France* into departments and cantons, and in the introduction of the new calendar, by which a strange metamorphosis has happened in the several portions of the year—for they bear an exact resemblance to the mathematical grades established among the associated clubs ;— they make a part of the same system of innovation, and were necessary to its completion. This affinity also forms a conspicuous feature in the exterior policy of *France*. The maxim of these societies— *"that the* END *to be obtained sanctifies the* MEANS *necessary to it,"* has been faithfully copied by the *Terrible Republic* in every stage of her eccentric progress. *"To divide and conquer"* is the motto inscribed on every page of her modern history. Her arms excite no unusual dread among nations. Before she aims the blow, she creates internal disorder—divides the people from their Government ; and then her purposes are easily effected by the bayonets of legionary cut-throats. Who will not weep at the fate of *Holland, Geneva, Switzerland,* and a great portion of *Italy* ? They mistook the poison for the honey—became the dupes of a perfidious policy—and then expired in the agonies at the feet of a directorial army. Prior to the disruption of the *French* fraternity among them, they were free and happy—now they are slaves and miserable. These once happy counties, not more fertile in animal and vegitable productions, than in the works of taste and genius, are now filled with blood and tears---their cities and temples are dismantled---their monuments of art and labor are levelled with the dust---their most precious memorials of antiquity are transported to *Paris*, and there deposited to amuse the curiosity of regicides, and mock-patriots---their religion and Government have fallen miserable victims to atheism and bondage ;---and these deluded republics are now doomed to disclose a frightful image of barbarism, murder and desolation.

SUCH are the effects of revolutionary sentiments. And does the bloated republic of *Liberty* and *Equality* exhibit a more pleasing picture ? GOD in his wrath has exposed her to strong delusions—permitted her to be the scourge of nations, and the instrument of her own destruction. A mild and pacific monarch, the father of his people—the hoary systems of national and municipal laws, and the venerable institutions of religion and morality, have all been destroyed by the philosophers of regenerated *France*. And what are the substitutes ? A prostituted Directory, whose bloody robes of office are an exact index to the cruel and relentless purpose of their hearts ;—a constitution, replete with absurdity, and founded on the modern rights of man—calculated to patronize ignorance and error at the expense of wisdom and truth---to banish able and upright men from the public councils, and to fill their places with the worthless demagogues of faction ;---a legal sanction to atheism and vice, and to the prevalence of blasphemous principles. The temples of the most high, and the various walks of science, once filled with devotion, and with the pupils of the arts, are now turned into military academies, and exhibit the awful apparatus of death. Where once stood the stately harvest, the joy and comfort of the peasant, *now waves a forest of bayonets.* The face of the earth, instead of flowers and blossoms of vegetation, is covered with the bones of immolated citizens ; and instead of pity at the terrible effusion of human blood, each wanton butchery of thousands produces a decree from the Directory, " *that the armies of the Republic have deserved well of their country!*" We turn with disgust and horror from this picture of human wretchedness, and solicit heaven in mercy to shield *America* from similar calamities.

IN *France*, under the monarchy, as well as under the republic, an invariable disposition has existed to acquire an undue ascendancy over us ; and this she seemed to consider as no more than an equivalent for our debt of national gratitude. Not till our Independence was fully guaranteed by the Convention of *Saratoga*, could she be prevailed on to assist us in our revolutionary war ; and the assistance she finally afforded us was not intended to establish our Independence, but to humble the pride of *England*. When the British Councils signified their disposition for peace, and their readiness to relinquish all claim of supremacy over us, *France* endeavored, by her insidious policy, to prevent a suspension of hostilities, and the adjustment of national disputes. By her diplomatic skill, she even induced Congress to instruct our Ministers not to conclude a peace without her consent, nor without an agreement on her part to the conditions of it. Her object was, if possible, to render this country dependent on its ally ; or if this project failed, to acquire an exclusive right to our fisheries—to some of our frontier posts, and to a large proportion of our western territory. Unable to corrupt the integrity of our Ministers;* she endeavored to

---

* The vigilance of Messrs. ADAMS and JAY is here only meant. Dr. FRANKLIN gave his utmost support to the views of the *French* cabinet —and why ? Let facts decide. When he entered into public life he possessed only a moderate share of property. During the many years he resided in *France*, in quality of minister, the expenses of his table were much

elude their vigilance by a perfidious attempt secretly to persuade *England* to claim the surrender of these privileges to herself—to insist on the return of the banished tories—on a restitution of their confiscated property, and total relinquishment of the Mississippi to the King of Spain. In this subtle manouvre, her object was, either to get these important advantages into the hands of *England* or *Spain*, or divided between them ; in which case she conceived herself able, by conquest or exchange, eventually to obtain the possession of them. But the die was already cast. The English cabinet, disgusted at the duplicity of a rival nation, instructed its Minister to conclude a secret or separate peace ; and our national interests dictated to our Ministers the necessity of an immediate negotiation, without the knowledge or concurrence of *France*. On this ground the treaty of 1783 was concluded ; and its conclusion afforded a temporary suspension to the intrigues of the French councils.

ANTERIOR to this event, in 1778, was adopted the treaty between *France* and *America*. As a reciprocity of benefits was the basis of the negotiation, it was stipulated at the desire of the French Minister, " *that free ships should make free goods* ;" or, in other words, that the goods of an enemy on board of the vessel of a friend, should not be liable to seizure or condemnation. The operation of this principle was found convenient, and similar stipulations are inserted in many modern treaties ; and, as between the contracting parties, the law of nations, relative to this point, is totally changed--- for by this law the goods on an enemy, found in neutral bottoms, are deemed lawful prize. But such is the extensive commerce, and maritime greatness of *England*,

---

above his salary : Indeed he lived in great splendor in *Paris*, while Mr. AD AMS, in order to support himself by his salary, was obliged to avoid expense, and for this purpose resided mostly in the country. After all this, Dr. FRANK-LIN left a princely fortune behind him at his death ! We wish not to blast the memory of the dead ;—these facts, however, are necessary to explain his equivocal conduct at the conclusion of the peace in 1783 that to govern herself by the more ancient rule, is strongly urged by her interest. Hence, the principle *"that free ships shall make free goods,"* is excluded from her policy, and the goods of an enemy, found by her cruisers in neutral vessels, may be legally seized and condemned : Yet notwithstanding this, *France* was bound to respect all treaty stipulations, and to permit our vessels to be the carriers of the goods of an enemy. This, however, was found to operate against the interest of the *Terrible Republic,* and she contrived pretexts to infract her engagements. The property of belligerents on board our vessels was seized and condemned as lawful prize. She resorted to our treaty with *England* in 1794, in justification of *past* excesses, as well as to authorize all *subsequent* depredations ;---by the rage of which our lawful commerce has been made the sport of licensed robbers---our industrious seamen imprisoned, and treated with indignity, and vast multitudes of them massacred in cool blood, by the modern cannibals of *France.* Her decrees on this subject, form an eccentric and multifarious code ; and, like those of the first legislator of *Athens,* are written in blood. By one of them, all the provisions and military stores of our own, bound to the port of a belligerent, and every species of property belonging to an enemy, and found on board of our vessels, were declared lawful prize. This is repugnant to the express stipulations of our treaty, and contrary to the law of nations---for by the one, the quality of the property is to be determined by the quality of the bottoms, and the other permits neutrals to furnish belligerent with these articles of commerce---provided blockaded ports, and places previously declared in a state of siege, draw no immediate supplies from them.---By a second, the cruisers of the republic were authorized to observe towards neutrals the same treatment which they suffered *England* to inflict.---By a third, the mere SUSPICION of her cruisers, that our vessels were laden with the property of an enemy, was declared good cause of capture and condemnation---unless the claimants were able to prove, that it did NOT belong to a belligerent.

TO prove an allegation *true*, and to adduce evidence of its *falsity*, are very opposite in their nature. Indeed, this decree exposed our merchants to this alternative, either to abandon their property to a gang of sea marauders, or to prove a negative before the sanguinary tribunals of the republic---a mode of process contrary to the maxims of every civilized nation---and an imposition not even practiced among savages.---By a fourth, the Directory has manifested to the world the *neplus ultra* of human depravity : Our citizens taken on board of belligerent vessels, are deemed PIRATES ; and are not even permitted to adduce either terror or violence as any excuse for an involuntary act. This decree, more bloody than the rescript of a NERO, evinces the blackest turpitude of Directorial policy, and that the *Terrible Republic* is now in the backward path to her ancient Gothicism. By numerous other decrees, all predicated on the principle of plunder and rapine, every portion of our extensive commerce has been prostrated ; and as long as the spoil is divided among the members of the Directory---the several courts and agents of the republic---we can expect no mitigation of these outrageous excesses.

ADD to this---the general policy of *France* is not confined to European nations, and to her own nautical banditti, but it also excites and supports a band of secret agents and *precious* friends in this country. What was the conduct of the infamous GENET, (and he literally pursued his instructions) but a tissue of misdemeanor, corruption and treason ? Did he not engage our citizens to fight the nations with whom we were at peace ? Did he not assume the right of opening our ports to the reception of prizes, and of fiting out privateers among us, to cruize against our friends ? Did he not claim the establishment of an independent and separate judiciary in the bosom of our country ? When informed by the President, that these practices were not authorized by treaty---that they were repugnant to the law of nations, and infractions of our neutral duties---

did he not with studied insolence appeal from the decision of that venerable magistrate to the opinion of the people ? Did he not establish secret and inflammable societies among us---inflate them with the poison of a *Parisan* mob---excite the prejudices of the people against their own Government---and implant in the bosom of *America*, the revolutionary dagger of *Europe* ? Were not the diplomatic intrigues of his successors in office, of a similar cast ? Were not their labored manifestos, filled with acumen and invective, better calculated for a misguided people than for the dispassionate Executive of the United States ? Did they not infuse their political *mania* into our public councils ;---and may not the existence of a party---the tide of opposition to executive measures---and that evident predilection for French fraternity, be traced to the same polluted source ? In fine--have not the Agents of *France*, rich in the esteem of the Directory, and of our own defectious citizens, granted bribes to some, and to others favors and protections ? If this proud republic means to be just---if universal revolution be not her object---why trample on all the forms prescribed among nations, and reject our messengers of peace ? Negotiation was not consistent with the interest or character of *France*. She was well aware, that a scrutiny of her conduct would impair her credit, and unmask her to the world in all her ugliness and deformity. It was therefore her policy to create suspense---and to protract the moment when a definitive answer of reception or rejection became necessary---thereby to manifest the appearance of a pacific disposition, and to enable her cruisers to augment their stock of plunder. Probably the late farce about a new negotiation, owes its origin on the part of *France* to the same principle, and will doubtless terminate in the same manner. If her public councils are free from ministerial cupidity, why demand almost three hundred thousand dollars for the private purses of the Directors ? To pay one cent for the privilege of stating our complaints, is abject slavery ; and sooner than *America* should feel the chains of tributary vassalage, may her existence be blotted out from under the sun of Heaven !

THESE desultory remarks, my fellow-citizens, exhibits but a very imperfect picture of the conduct and views of *France*. The measures of that republic for most of the last eight years, have been so extraordinary in their nature, and so rapid in their succession, that they appear more like the shades of a magic lanthern, than the settled operations of any durable policy. Like the corruscations of the northern lights, they diverge into a profusion of lines, and emit no other rays than those of blood ; and if the prospect of a peaceful conclusion now and then breaks thro' the gloom, it results either from the projected union of all mankind against them, or from the probability of their own eventual explosion.

IT is a curious feature in the operation of our Government that, while danger like a cloud thickens over us, measures of *defense* against *France* are urged and pursued by one party, and against *England* measures of *offense* are as strongly promoted by the other. This diversity of sentiment and exertion, at this eventual crisis of liberty or bondage, must be imputed to the new political light of *France* : We not only feel its influence---but it is her boast---an engine with which she is almost sure to effect her purposes. What but this gave birth to the proposition in our public councils for the suspension of all commerce with *England*, and to the subsequent resolutions for the sequestration of British property ? What but this produced and invigorated the violent opposition to the treaty of 1794, with that kingdom ? This may be considered as the last *important* struggle of a deadly faction ; and the extraordinary manner in which it was generated and conducted, excited a temporary delirium in the public mind. It, however, verified the truth of an old observation, that sudden and powerful impressions generally give a wrong bias to public opinion, and that mature reflection will alone enable the great body of the people to discover their real interests. This remark might be illustrated by many examples. The treaties of *Utrecht* and *Sa-*

ville, in 1712 and 1729, created a similar ferment in *England*. The doors of the parliment-house were barricaded by the enraged multitude---the ministers who negotiated them were pelted in the streets, and burnt in effigy by an irritated populace---yet their eventual operation manifested their salutary tendency ; and it is under these two very treaties, in concert with the navigation act, that the English commerce has increased to almost a monopoly.

CONVINCED that perfidy and aggression accumulated strength from patient forbearance, *America* banished at last the dreams of confidence, and resorted to a system of defense---the origin of which may be traced in the rejection of our ministers. To prevent the sacrifice of our unprotected seamen, and the wanton pillage of our property, and at the same to force the republic to terms of accommodation, the treaty of 1778 was declared as no longer obligatory---all commercial intercourse with the French dominions was prohibited---an infant navy was established to convoy our merchantmen, and to capture the armed cruisers of the republic---our ports and harbors were fortified, and garrisoned with troops for the common defense, and provision made for an eventual army, equal to the exigency of the times.

INTERNAL security was also promoted by this system of defense. Our Government adopted measures to restrain the influence of defectious aliens, and to curb that *mendax infamia* from the press, which had corrupted public opinion---excited an opposition to the laws, and stimulated rebellion. Perhaps a concise analysis of some of these governmental measures may be expected at this time, and be deemed compatible with the duties of the day.

THE Alien and Sedition bills have been attacked as unconstitutional and oppressive : They have excited the complaint of defectious foreigners and citizens, and the pointed disapprobation of the Legislatures of two States in the Union.

THE Alien bill permits the President to order dangerous aliens to depart the United States ; and, in case of refusal, to cause them to be removed or imprisoned. This act is said to be unconstitutional, because it adopts a summary process, and deprives aliens of the right of trial by jury. These objections necessarily pre-suppose, that *removal* implies *punishment*, and consequently the actual commission of offenses ; and hence this preposterous conclusion is drawn, that punishments are authorized without the trial by jury. A very simple mode of argument will refute every possible objection to this act. In the first place, the constitution recognizes no principle as applicable to aliens. In the next place, aliens are not parties to this instrument, and therefore cannot claim the benefits of it. They possess not the rights of citizens, and therefore a removal deprives them of none. The law very wisely supports many of them to entertain sentiments of a hostile nature against the Government ; and therefore to prevent the actual commission of offenses, it authorizes their removal from the United States. Can this precautionary measure be deemed rigorous or unconstitutional ? Aliens are like travellers in a strange land ; they are exposed to the same inconveniences, and are equally limited in their rights---mere tenants at sufferance under the Government. No traveller has a right to intrude himself into a strange family ; and if permitted by the laws of hospitality to refresh himself in it, he cannot claim a longer indulgence than the family is willing to give— particularly if he creates disorders, or manifests a disposition to hostility, the family has a right to rid itself of a troublesome guest. The United States are only a family on a more extensive scale ; they have a similar right to see, that the laws of political hospitality are not infracted, and to expel suspicious and dangerous itinerants from their jurisdiction. This is not a singular ex-

ercise of authority—every Government inherently possess the right to exercise it—and all Governments
have exercised it on the eve of a war, or when the
safety of the public demanded it.

EQUALLY weak, and capable of refutation, are the
arguments against the Sedition Bill. To constitute an
offense under that part of the act relative to libellous
publications, several requisites are necessary. The mat-
ter published must be *false, scandalous* and *malicious*—di
rectly tend to *defame* the President, or one of the branch-
es of the federal Legislature---and to bring one or the
other of them into *contempt* and *disrepute*. This clause
is objected to, as repugnant to that article of the constitution, which very wisely provides, "*that no law shall
be made abridging the liberty of speech or of the press.*"
This sound maxim constituted one article in the political creed of our ancestors—and it has been in practice
ever since the year 1694. This practice, in a great
measure regulated by various judicial decisions, and by
the concurrent opinion of learned sages, has given to
these words a technical operation—a precise and defi-
native meaning---which is, *that no law shall be made to pro-
hibit publications.* Were such a law in existence, the liberty of speech and of the press, would be abridged---
but to punish the authors of false and malicious libels,
which tend to destroy the characters of public men---
to disunite the people, and to bring the Government into contempt, is to invigorate and enlarge the boundary
of its freedom. All crimes are founded in the abuse
of the liberty of action ; and is it unconstitutional to restrain this abuse by the imposition of adequate penalties ? The same argument would come with equal force
from the mouths of robbers and traitors---with equal
propriety they might complain of the abridgment of
their liberty by the infliction of criminal justice. Some
pretend to argue that the Sedition Law, in the punishment of libellers, creates a new crime in society. The
fact is, that this description of offenders were before
punishable by the common law of the land---but as au-

thors, by the common law, were not permitted to al-
ledge the truth of libellous publications as an excuse,
the act in question allows it to be given in evidence ;
and this is one reason which induced Congress to pass
it. The common law also confided the nature and extent of the punishment to the discretion of the Court---
but the Sedition Law defines it ; and this is another
reason which prompted the federal Legislature to enact
a statute on the subject. Besides---most of our state
Constitutions contain clauses similar to the one in our
federal charter, "*that no law shall be made abridging the
liberty of speech or of the press* ;" and yet all the state
courts have recognized the doctrine of libels---and have,
at their discretion, inflicted penalties on the authors of
libellous publications. It is therefore a curious kind of
argument, and pregnant with absurdity, to say, that the
state courts have a right to admit this common law
principle, and at the same time to deny its operation in
the courts of the Union---for the federal and local constitutions contain the same prohibitory clause, and expressed in the very same words.

THESE two Acts of Congress originated in the necessity of the times, and were found highly expedient.

MOST of our domestic troubles for several years
past---our divisions both in and out of our public councils, are very justly ascribed to the restless temper of
aliens ; they have fomented and nourished discontents---
impaired public confidence, and awakened treasonable
practices. Many of them are fugitives of justice ; and
the more securely to propagate their revolutionary sen-
timents---the very *momentum* of their nature---they have
taken refuge in the United States. So true is the sar-
casm of a foreign satyrist, that in *America*, "*every
scoundrel convict is a King!*"

SEVERAL venal and prostituted presses have long
labored among us with the most detestable views. To support
the liberty of the press, must base calumny and

lies be tolerated ? Is this liberty infringed when the
murderers of reputation, and the propagators of rebellion and treason, are exposed to the rod of punishment ? Our Government, like every other of a representative nature, derives its energy and support from
public opinion ; and when this fails, or becomes corrupted, it either degenerates to a phantom, or is totally destroyed. Public opinion, in this country, is formed and regulated by the presses. These are the mirrors
in which the people see and judge of the conduct of
their rulers. If therefore these important mediums of
communication prove deceptive, and are pregnant with
inflammatory and revolutionary sentiments---if they sacrifice the most palpable truths to the most destructive
falshoods, and thereby disseminate groundless jealousies,
and weaken the hands of Government---is it not the
the duty of our political watchmen to punish aggressors in
the abuse of constitutional liberty ? A deluge of the
blackest calumny has for years issued from some of our
public papers, and eventually excited an irritation in
the public mind. The impression at first was hardly
perceptible---but the continual dropping of the water-
spout will in time wear away the most durable substance.
The President has been painted as a sullen tyrant---the
majorities in Congress as the prostituted hirelings of
the British cabinet, and the fraternizing brotherhood of
French partizans among us as the great pillars of our
insulted liberty, and as the saviours of our country.
To these very partizans we may charge all our political
troubles. Their actions authorize all the high carnival of
rebellion and of revolution, and serve to create a horde
of domiciliary tyrants and cut-throats in *America* : For,
while our constituted authorities have struggled to support a system of neutrality, they by a repellant power,
have aimed to draw us into a contest with *England*,
and to bring us under the yoke of Directorial despotism. Our policy and interest dictate the necessity of
peace---but these proud sons of sedition, subservient to
the beck of the brutes and the atheists of *France*, dissemi-

nate their licentious and poisonous dogmas---disaffect the public mind---paralyze the exertions of Government---and patronize on the American stage the bloody tragedies of *Europe.*

A DOCTRINE is prevalent, and dexterously propagated as the great palladium of our liberty, that the people ought to keep alive the fire of republican jealousy, and to watch with an eye of suspicion every measure of our Government. This is constitutionally right to a certain extent---but when they imagine, that our Government *naturally* inclines to corruption, and to a dangerous accumulation of power, they manifest inaccurate conceptions of its structure and principles. No political truth is more evident than that foreign Governments are pregnant with danger---while the greatest danger to be apprehended in *America,* is from the wicked disposition, and blind credulity, of certain portions of the people. These contrary and opposite sources of danger arise from the different natures of the several Governments. European institutions are not composed of a delegation of power ;---the constituted authorities are not responsible to the people for an abuse of trust ; they possess a distinct and separate interest from their constituents ; and such is the opulence and power of privileged orders, that the community is in a manner controlled by them. This opulence and power, and this control, in *America,* are wholly in the hands of the people. Our rulers, at very limited periods, return to the walks of private life---submit their conduct to the scrutiny of their constituents, on the rectitude of which they rely for the continuance of public suffrage--and the burthens they impose on the community are equally felt by themselves. If these remarks be just, it necessarily results, that the grand pillar of foreign Governments, is POWER, and that the only foundation of our own is PUBLIC CONFIDENCE. One other conclusion is equally obvious, that foreign Governments possess a *dangerous power*, and that a simi-

lar power, in this country, *is wholly vested in the people.*
A well-constructed fortress is sometimes impregnable---
but public opinion is as variable as the winds of Heaven. These sentiments may possibly excite the surprize
of some, and perhaps others may consider them as a
species of political blasphemy---but the truth of them
is verified by the history of other nations, and by the
constant experience of our own.

OF all the calamities to which nations are exposed,
those of war are the most cruel and destructive.---Yet,
like many other evils in society, they must rather be mi-
tigated than expunged from the system of human policy. We need not here repeat the distinctions usually
made by civilians between the wars designated by the terms
just and *unjust*---because they all agree, that if any may
be termed *just*, they are those of a defensive nature---
and because no other description of war will ever be
consistent either with our interest or policy. If therefore *America* draws the sword, it will not be to plunder,
nor to conquer, nor to enslave and to inflict misery on
the human race---but to repel aggravated aggressions,
and to snatch our Independence from the meretricious
embraces of French fraternity, or to save it from the
iron grasp of undisguised and open enemies.

IF an invasion of our country takes place, or if rebellion be excited by the arts and intrigues of foreign
cabinets, or by their secret and authorized agents, we
may anticipate a resistance adequate to the danger.
The military spirit manifested in all part of the Union,
affords a happy presage of success. Every day brings
tidings of additional corps, who have voluntarily ten-
dered their services to our country ; and the one in this
town, and now before us, is not the least respectable,
nor the last to manifest American patriotism. Let each
individual member of it bear in mind, that in proportion to the toils and dangers of the field, is the glory to
be acquired ; and that the reward of essential services,

in times of public hazard, is a harvest of laurels. One prominent feature in the duty of soldiers, is to guard and to protect the standard, round which they rally. The loss of it often exhibits the want of courage ; and to desert it, is absolute disgrace. Motives of a peculiar nature concur to stamp the one attached to the FEDER-AL VOLUNTEERS OF PORTLAND, with additional value.* It is the workmanship of female hands ; and the donation originated in female patriotism. These circumstances will stimulate, fresh from the mint of miitary honor, the brightest deeds of glory in its defense.

WERE men restricted to the weapons furnished them by nature, the concomitants of war would be less dreadful. It is to the prostitution of their intelligent faculties, and perhaps to their deadly hatred of each other, that we must impute those terrible instruments of death, to which they always resort in the settlement of national disputes, and frequently in the adjustment of private injuries. They are the inventors of these dreadful engines---from whose brazen mouths issue frightful peals of thunder, and volumes of smoke and lightning--- whose ponderous messengers, swift-winged in air, drench fields in blood---involve whole cities in flame and dust, and sink the proudest navies beneath the wave. The ingenuity of mankind has, therefore, reduced war to a science---in which personal prowess and bravery are poor substitutes for military equipment and discipline. Hence it is our duty to acquire the theory of modern war, and to be prepared to practice its lessons in the field.

---

* The PORTLAND FEDERAL VOLUNTEERS, is a company composed of the Youth of this town. Its Officers are commissioned, and its services accepted, by the President of the *United States*, in conformity to the Act of Congress, passed the 28th May 1798.—On the 25th of June 1799, the Young LADIES of the town presented the FEDERAL VOLUNTEERS with an elegant Standard. — This badge of female patriotism was accompanied by an Address at once laconic and impressive. The ceremony on the part of the LADIES was conducted with the greatest propriety ; – and the military evolutions of the day reflected the highest honor on the VOLUNTEERS.

BUT here let me pause ———— While *Europe*, like
some fiery volcano, trembles with frightful and protract-
ed eruptions, and the night-bird pays her devoirs over
hecatombs of slain, Peace, with her numerous blessings,
is still predominant in our country. The danger an-
nouced from the bosom of that low hung cloud on the
margin of the east, decreases in proportion to the strength
of our defensive measures ; and we trust that, on the
face of this great empire, perpetual tranquility is stamp-
ed with the finger of heaven. Let us learn wisdom
from the calamities of war, and read the projected fate
of *America* in those prominent lessons, written in the
blood of nations.

PROMOTE the progress of education among the
people, and encourage the arts and sciences. These are
at once the ornaments and glory of a Republic. Hence
will proceed wise legislators, and good laws, and an unity
of sentiment in the public mind. Fortified with these
ramparts, we may bid defiance to the thunders of the
most potent attack, and extort a pre-eminent respect
from the world.

ALREADY our opulence and extent of country have
attracted the notice of the most distant nations. "Where
rolls the sea on which our sails have not been spread---
and where is the clime not enriched by the productions
of our soil?" The great fabric of our constitution and
laws, founded in the patient deliberation of an enlight-
ened people, is considered by other nations of the most
perfect model of political wisdom and precision. Its
pillars, composed of the American virtues, will only
moulder and fall in the prevalence of disunion and corruption. Then suffer not the canker-worm of jealousy
to weaken them, nor let the proverb of old be verified,
that the unusual prosperity of a nation announces the
period of its fall. The means of safety and happiness
are within ourselves. We have little to fear from the
open violence of outward enemies : Their secret influ-

ence, effected by their gold and insidious arts, is most to
be dreaded. Who is proof against the charms of opulence and power ? Probity and honor are sometimes pur-
loined by the hand of *Midas*, and virtue and integrity
banished by corruption and pride : But, altho' a SUMNER,
one of the brightest ornaments of human nature, has
been recently snatched from our local councils, still we
have an ADAMS to concert, and a WASHINGTON to ex-
ecute, the measures of national defence ; and therefore
we need not fear the arts of flattery, nor be intimidated
by the menaces of opposition.

IF our conduct be actuated by sound policy, and if
we cling to our constitution as the rock of our political
salvation, we may safely calculate on the events of futu-
rity. The broad perspective of time is expanded to our
view. The margins of our interior waters are crowded
with cities, and spires of magnificent structures are
buried in the clouds. The gloomy forests, once the re-
sidence of savage beasts, and unexplored by human
steps, now exhibit peaceful mansions, and the plenteous
fruits of culture. Our canvass whitens the *Arctic* seas,
and swells to the breezes of the torrid zone. Smiling
peace, and roseate health, establish their salutary reign ;
and the prospects of pleasure beyond the grave, mitigate the terrors of dissolution.

O HAPPY ——— thrice happy Country ! ——— Pos-
essed of opulance and power ——— May thy happiness be
perpetual !

Reprinted by Robert Stoddard Publishing
2019
Every effort has been made to duplicate the original work and to respect authenticity.
Grammar, spelling, punctuation and formatting are as original.
Any errors in this reprint are intentional.

The following biography of Amos Stoddard is taken from the book,
The Autobiography Manuscript of Major Amos Stoddard

Biography of Amos Stoddard

The author of this oration, Amos Stoddard, was a veteran of the American Revolution and the War of 1812. He was a lawyer, an author, and a soldier. He was an American patriot. Amos Stoddard is mostly remembered in American history with the transfer of the upper Louisiana at St. Louis in May 1804. Stoddard County, Missouri was named to honor him as the first governor and first civil commandant of the upper Louisiana.

Amos Stoddard was born in Woodbury, Connecticut on October 26, 1762. His father moved the family to Massachusetts in 1765. He initially purchased a farm in Lanesborough and then another farm 10 miles south in Lenox in February 1773. It was at Lenox that Amos came of age.

In the spring of 1779, at the age of 16, Amos began asking his father for permission to join the army. His father finally relented. Amos enlisted at Lenox and reported to West Point. There he mustered-in with Inspector General Baron de Steuben. He left us his recollection of the event:

> *"On our arrival the recruits were drawn up to be inspected by the Baron De Steuben. Fearing that my undersize would induce him to reject me, I gradually gathered the dirt under my heals—and when he arrived opposite to me in the line he asked me several questions and finally said, "perhaps you may do"—and at the same time putting the hilt of his sword under my chin saying, "you must learn to hold up your head!" The hun eye and fierce countenance of the Baron, together with the large star glittering on his breast, in some measure terrified me, and caused a trembling in my limbs."*

Amos started his service in the infantry but later served in the artillery under the command of Capt. Henry Burbeck, where, according to Amos, *"We experienced as much enjoyment as usually falls to the lot of Soldiers."* In 1781, he served under the overall command of Major General Marquis de Lafayette and participated in the siege of Yorktown from September 28 until October 19, 1781. After the surrender ceremony, Amos, as a member of a small detachment, marched into Yorktown and lowered the British colors and raised the Stars and Stripes.

At the end of the War, Amos returned to Lenox. Thus began Amos Stoddard's civilian quest to determine his course in life. At first he taught school at Lenox for a year and one half. In 1784, he went to Boston to receive his military pay. An encounter along the way brought him to the attention of Charles Cushing (the brother of William Cushing, the first associate justice of the Supreme Court of the United States) who offered him a job as a clerk in the Supreme Judicial Court of Massachusetts in Boston. His work as a clerk was interrupted in December 1786 when he enlisted for military service for the purpose of suppressing Shays' Rebellion. He served until the end of 1787. He then briefly returned to his court clerk duties in Boston before deciding to make the law his profession.

Amos began studying law under the tutelage of Judge Seth Padleford at Taunton, Massachusetts circa 1790. His law study was interrupted in December 1790 so Amos could take a trip to London, England in order to try to secure an estate for his uncle. He spent eights months in London, published one book there, and returned in the autumn 1791 and completed his law studies. He passed the Bar and was admitted an attorney in February 1796. He then relocated to Hallowell, Massachusetts, (today Hallowell, Maine) where he served several sessions as the representative in the state legislature. During this time he also became a founding member of the Masonic Lodge at Hallowell and gave an oration to its members on St. John's Day in 1797.

Amos described himself as having a "roving disposition." He apparently quickly became bored with his sedentary life as a lawyer. On February 13, 1797, he wrote to Hon. William Cushing about his interest in an overseas position in government, requesting that the associate justice bring his name to the attention of the "executive," President Adams. This is probably what led to his name being submitted to the U.S. Senate by President Adams and his commission as a captain in the 2nd U.S. Regiment of Artillerists & Engineers in May 1798. He had now traded his quiet civilian life as a lawyer for the ranks of the military. Amos spent the next four years commanding seaport fortifications at Portland, Newport, and Portsmouth. Captain Amos Stoddard delivered his Independence Day oration while he was in command at Fort Sumner at Portland.

By the fall of 1802, Amos likely grew wearisome of seafort command and sought a new and more challenging assignment. He brought his desire to the attention of his military masters and in December 1802 he was ordered to lead a company of artillerists west to Fort Fayette at Pittsburgh. After several months of gathering supplies he was ordered to "*descend the Ohio River and ascend the Mississippi River to Kaskaskia*" below St. Louis.

As it turned out, Capt. Stoddard was serving as an advance force in anticipation of a westward expedition being led by Meriwether Lewis and William Clark. Stoddard rendezvoused with Lewis and Clark at Kaskaskia on November 28, 1803. The United States had by then already publicly announced the signing of an agreement for the acquisition of the Louisiana Territory from France. Capt. Amos Stoddard was then commissioned the first civil commandant of upper Louisiana.

Capt. Stoddard and his artillery company crossed the Mississippi River and marched into St. Louis on March 9, 1804, where Amos Stoddard, representing the Republic of France, presided over the transfer of the territory from Spain to France. Then, on March 10, 1804, on behalf of the United States, he accepted the territory from France to the United States. His representation on behalf of the Republic of France is ironic considering the disagreeable content and spirit of his remarks towards France in his Independence Day oration in 1799.

On May 21, 1804, Captain Amos Stoddard escorted Capt. Meriwether Lewis to St. Charles where he saw the Corp. of Discovery set-off on their journey up the Missouri River and ultimately to the Pacific Ocean. Before the expedition departed, Amos Stoddard wrote an agency agreement and was appointed the agent for Meriwether Lewis during his absence.

Amos Stoddard was replaced as governor by William Henry Harrison on October 1, 1804. In the fall of 1805, he led a group of Indian chiefs to Washington. Captain Stoddard then took furlough due to illness until the fall of 1806. He then raised a new company of recruits and was assigned duty at Newport Barracks and Fort Adams in the Mississippi Territory, and later in command at Fort Dearborn in Chicago. It was during this time, on June 30, 1807, that Amos Stoddard was promoted to major.

In the fall of 1808, Major Stoddard again took furlough to conduct research along the Mississippi and Red rivers for a book he was desiring to write. In December 1809, he was in command at Fort Columbus on Governor's Island in New York harbor. Already a member of the U.S.M.P.S., Stoddard joined the New York Historical Society and used this time to complete work on his book, *Sketches, Historical and Descriptive, of Louisiana.* He also re-wrote the work of Tadeusz Kosciusko and published the first drill and tactics training manual for the U.S. artillery, *Exercise for Garrison and Field Ordinance Together with Maneuvers.*

From September until Christmas 1811, Major Stoddard was a member of a general court martial for General James Wilkinson held at Fredericktown. This was the first of two court martial trials for Wilkinson. He was acquitted at both. After this service, Major Stoddard was assigned to the War Department in Washington.

Shortly after war was declared on England on June 18, 1812, Major Stoddard accepted an appointment from Secretary of War William Eustis as deputy quartermaster under the commissary general of ordinance, Decius Wadsworth. However, as events quickly unfolded in the war, and with defeats and setbacks mounting, Major Stoddard was also asked to provide intelligence and council to the secretary of war. On August 20, 1812, he submitted his *"Outlines of a Plan for an Attack on Canada"* to Secretary Eustis. In September, he was ordered to Pittsburgh to command a forward supply base for the northwestern army. By November, with the situation of the war becoming even more tentative, he was ordered to *join* the northwestern army under the overall command of William Henry Harrison, an army comprised of militia units of which he expressed no confidence.

In June 1804, as the first civil commandant of the upper Louisiana, Amos Stoddard wrote the following to his mother:

> *"A military man never knows what to depend on.*
> *He must always be ready to move when duty calls, and to*
> *consider his time and talents as the property of the public."*

Such was the case when Major Stoddard was ordered to join the northwestern army under General Harrison. He regretfully obeyed the orders. Major Amos Stoddard rendezvoused with the army at the Maumee River about the first of February, 1813.

At the Maumee River, the army began work on a wooden fortification that was later named Fort Meigs. The army at Fort Meigs consisted mostly of Virginia and Kentucky militia units and only a few hundred U.S. Army regulars. General Harrison departed the encampment but unwisely left Virginia militia Brigadier General Joel Leftwich in charge of the completion of the fort. Disaster then ensued. Torrential rains began. The men stayed in their tents and did nothing to complete the fort—and the general did nothing to compel them to work. Their enlistments being up, the militia men then left for home on April 1st—and with a British army approaching left the others to their fate. As the senior officer, Major Stoddard then took command on April 2, 1813.

Major Amos Stoddard was only in command for 10 days— yet he was able to instill discipline, rally the men and complete construction of the fort. Militia men totally unfamiliar with artillery and cannon were quickly trained to man and fire the guns. When the British army arrived across the river and their artillery batteries were constructed on ground higher, it was apparent that the men in the fort were extremely vulnerable. The idea to construct a "Grand Traverse" 20 feet deep across the interior of the fort was probably conceived by Major Stoddard based on his siege experience at Yorktown during the American Revolution. The work on the trench was obscured from the view of the British by canvas tents placed in front of it. The dirt was piled up facing the enemy guns. When the tents were removed, the British were astonished to see that the men in the trench were nearly completely protected from the fire of their shot and shells.

The British began their artillery attack on the fort in the early hours of May 1st and didn't stop firing until night. Two were killed and four were injured on that first day. One of the injured was Major Stoddard. He received his wound from a shell that exploded over the Grand Battery where he was commanding fire.

Major Amos Stoddard died from the symptoms of tetanus at 11:00 pm on the night of May 11, 1813. He was buried the next day by the men of the 2nd U.S. Regiment of Artillery in front of the Grand Battery at the place he sustained his injury. A large, granite commemorative marker has been erected near that location at Fort Meigs Historical Site in Ohio in his memory.

To Order Additional Copies, Contact:
Robert Stoddard Publishing
rob.stoddard@hotmail.com

www.ingramcontent.com/pod-product-compliance
Lightning Source LLC
Chambersburg PA
CBHW072157020426
42334CB00018B/2057